Monkeys

MONKEYS

Monkeys in the Animal World

The king of the apes proclaims his superiority at the top of his voice.
Despite its impressive appearance, the gorilla is a perfectly harmless vegetarian.

Four remarkable great apes

The chimpanzee, the gorilla and the orangutan are the three giants of the ape and monkey world. Large in size, intelligent, and civilized in their behaviour, these apes are anthropoids – resembling human beings – as are gibbons, who owe their inclusion in this category of primates to their upright stance.

A mother's tenderness for her child. Among chimpanzees, the bonds between mother and child are very strong: females care for their offspring for many years.

Chimpanzees spend 30 to 50 percent of their time on the ground. Although they are built more for an arboreal life, these apes often play and picnic on the ground.

Perched high out of reach, chimpanzees can cock a snook at predators.

Among the 200 species of apes and monkeys found across the world, a small group stands out for its striking resemblance to human beings. This is the family of the great apes, which includes the chimpanzee, the gorilla and the orangutan. Body outline, facial expressions, behaviour and social life – many aspects of these primates are strangely reminiscent of humans. What could be more natural, since 90 percent of their genetic make-up is the same as that of humans.

Members of the human race? That is the question scientists wrestled with when faced with the belated discovery of the pygmy chimpanzee.

Chimpanzee's have very expressive faces. This elderly male seems lost in thought, but he's able to smile, and even laugh.

Disconcerting agility

Thanks to its long arms, the generally slender and graceful chimpanzee can hang and move through the trees with enormous ease. This comes in handy when you have to build your nest among the foliage each evening. Even the heavier orangutan leads an essentially arboreal life, and though it may be slower than the chimpanzee at leaping from branch to branch, it nonetheless moves with agility and precision. In the super-heavyweight class,

Even old orangutans perform acrobatics in the trees.

The gorilla is the largest primate alive on Earth today. Handicapped by its great bulk, it rarely climbs into the trees and prefers to stay on the ground.

though, the gorilla refrains from these sorts of games. An adult gorilla weighs almost 300 kilograms and can stand up to 1.7 metres tall when in an upright position with its knees slightly bent.

Two Africans and an Asian

The great apes are unknown in the Americas, Europe and Australia. Chimpanzees are found in the wild in the forests of equatorial Africa, while lowland and mountain gorillas inhabit the

With age, gorillas may suffer problems of hair-loss.

The mountain gorilla is most often to be found on the steep hillsides of the Central African massifs where it enjoys an abundant food supply.

The orangutan can satisfy its appetite with the immense variety of plant species of Sumatra and Borneo. An accomplished botanist, it knows where to find the best plants.

A mother orangutan and her baby in the tropical jungle.

western part of Central Africa. As for the orangutan, it is the only great ape of Asia where its once vast territory is now confined solely to the virgin forest of Sumatra and Borneo.

Eyesight comparable to that of humans

The senses of the great apes are very like our own. Although their sense of smell is poor, their eyesight is very highly developed. As with all primates, the eyes are situated in the front of the head rather than on either side of the face and this particular forward-looking arrangement enables them to see in relief. Chimpanzees' and gorillas' eyes are protected by very prominent eyebrow arches, while in the case of the orangutan these 'bumpers' disappear to give the face a more benign appearance. In any case the apes of these three families are the only ones to look their fellow-creatures straight in the eye: other animals generally avoid the gaze of others of their kind.

The stormy life of the chimpanzee

The features of the orangutan express all the gentleness of this peaceable animal.

All the great apes live in social structures governed by precise rules. Chimpanzees are sedentary, and gather together in social groups ranging from a couple of dozen individuals up to a hundred or even more. From generation to generation they remain within the boundaries of their clan territory which covers some 20 square kilometres. If strangers enter the territory they are chased away with a chorus of angry cries as the chimpanzees strike the ground and shake the branches in an attempt to frighten the intruders. During the ordinary course of events, little

This young gorilla already has a determined gaze. The sharply jutting eyebrow arches give it an air of severity, even though this is just a peaceful leaf-eater.

▼ Twenty-three different cries have been distinguished in the chimpanzee's repertoire: they are without contest the noisiest animals in the forest. Their grimaces are more eloquent still; thanks to their mobile features they have the greatest range of facial expressions in the animal kingdom. The chimpanzee pouts its lips when begging, breaks into a sort of smile with all its teeth hidden as a sign of submission, and employs the same smile but with the teeth showing when faced with a dominant individual.

Troops of chimpanzees engage in boisterous discussion groups amidst the forest greenery. Grooming sessions are accompanied by animated cries and murmurs.

The orangutan's arms are so long it hardly knows what to do with them!

groups within this noisy community form, break up again and re-form as the mood takes them.

The gorilla family group

Groups of gorillas rarely have more than ten members – usually with females in the majority. Throughout the day the family of gorillas is constantly on the move looking for food: leaves, berries, young shoots and certain types of bark. They travel 1 or 2 kilometres a day in this way, covering an area which amounts to some 5 to 10 square kilometres a year. When food is scarce, gorillas extend their range in order to survive.

Anarchists in the forest

The orangutans are much more solitary that the other great apes and their social structure follows less rigid rules. Generally speaking, groups of females and juveniles gravitate around large males and all of them find their own niche in the heart of the

Only the carefree young orangutans venture on to the ground.

Gorillas spend almost eight hours a day feeding. On a diet like that, it will not be long before this juvenile comes to look as imposing as its elders.

The undisputed leader among the gorillas is the 'silverback'. He watches over his troop, mainly made up of females. Other males of reproductive age are expelled from the group.

Apes and monkeys spend their time searching each other's coats for lice. However the purpose of grooming is not just to rid the animals' fur of parasites; more than a measure of hygiene, this has become a ritual which fosters friendship. This behaviour occupies a large part of the social life of all apes living in groups. Among gorillas, grooming sessions are much enjoyed by juveniles but are less common among adults.

This misshapen mask is that of the dominant male orangutan.

forest, forming a little community that then moves within a territory of about 1 to 5 square kilometres.

Age and sex command drastic changes in physical appearance

There are enormous physical differences between the sexes in the gorilla and the orangutan. When a male gorilla reaches sexual maturity towards the age of 15, his height and weight increase considerably. The chest becomes hairless and the coat on the back turns to whitish grey; these males are known as 'silverbacks'. Generally speaking there is only one silverback in a group of gorillas and he maintains the cohesion of the troop. In the case of the male orangutan, however, it is the face which changes completely: a growth in the shape of a half-moon appears on either side of the cheeks when the animal becomes dominant. Male gorillas and orangutans of reproductive age that come up against the diktat of another male already in place remain in a 'subadult' state. Devoid of silver back or facial disks, the pleasures of the flesh are forbidden to them, sometimes for a dozen years or more!

Mealtimes are usually a free-for-all among primates, but not among the chimpanzees: according to rank, they either make offerings or beg for a pittance.

The language of hierarchy

The dominant male plays the big shot and spends his time intimidating any other pretenders seeking to lay claim to his harem. Subjugated, a dominated male will give way before his leader, present his rear towards him in a suggestive manner and shower him with caresses to the lips, thighs or genitals. The dominant animal, among gorillas and orangutans, is the only one allowed to enjoy the favours of the females. Chimpanzees are more inclined to share,

Deep in concentration, the chimpanzee takes on a philosophical air.

The graceful body of the bonobo or pygmy chimpanzee recalls the outline of the human form. This 'near-human' will even adopt an upright stance in order to carry food.

A gorilla guards his kingdom with great care...and with great theatricality. When gorillas fight they conduct battles in slow motion and measure blows so as not to wound.

however, and although the dominant male reserves the right to choose those females with whom he wishes to mate he will not hesitate to ally himself with other males in order to strengthen his authority over the group, and these males will then be allowed to mate after him.

A great deal of play-acting and very little real fighting

Gorillas are very peaceable animals and fights are rare. When two silverbacks meet they put on impressive display

Chimpanzees enjoy smelling flowers before they eat them.

It's time for a break among the orangutans. These 'great red monkeys' can sleep easy, for in their natural habitat they have only one enemy: humans.

The orangutan practises his scales, striking panic into the forest.

designed to intimidate: they utter terrible cries, tear at the foliage as if mad with rage, draw themselves up in terrifying fashion, beat their chests violently and strike frenetically at the ground.

A great outcry in the jungle

Among orangutans there is no real fighting at all in the physical sense of the word: the dominant male utters a long howl which can be heard for several kilometres around. This cry, the most striking in the forests of

Chimpanzees often adopt voluptuous positions when they relax. The sexual organ is external in the primate unlike in most other animals.

Usually rather irritable, the silverbacks soon lose all their reserve when faced with a playful juvenile.

Asia, terrifies the other males who keep their distance. Chimpanzees too are very noisy as they romp about, but they are much more bellicose than orangutans. A simple scuffle, for example, can develop into a bloody duel with individuals wounded and sometimes even killed.

The peaceable females

The female great apes have no say in these matters though the forest is alive with their chattering voices. It has been

This female bonobo turns the heads of all her admirers.

observed in the different communities that the females have no fixed hierarchy and generally speaking it is the mothers of newborn babies who lay down the law.

The unbridled sexuality of the pygmy chimpanzee

The pygmy chimpanzee or bonobo is sexually active throughout the year. Unlike other animals which confine their love-making to reproductive periods alone, bonobos may assuage their sexual needs every day. Another singular trait is the fact that they mate face to face (as orangutans occasionally do). Bonobos have a range of highly elaborate erotic games and have transformed their sexuality into a veritable code of social behaviour. Mating usually takes place before meals, for example, and whenever there is any risk of confrontation within the group. By this means the pygmy chimpanzees work up an appetite and avoid any conflict.

Love, love forever…

For the heavyweights among the great apes, matters of love take a more usual form: the mating of the gorilla tends to be slow,

Bonobos have a reputation for being sex-mad, but there's no lack of tenderness.

Baby gorillas develop twice as fast as their human counterparts – which is just as well, since they weigh only 1.5 kilograms at birth: half the weight of a human baby.

Throughout infancy, the only face a young orangutan sees is that of its mother. It is only when they reach adolescence, towards the age of seven, that orangutans come together in groups. During this period the juveniles chase each other around and engage in mock-battles. Chimpanzees orm groups earlier and organize 'crèches' in which a dozen young apes are watched over by one or two mothers. Juveniles establish their place in the group through play.

Riding piggy back on its mother's back, this young gorilla can enjoy an introductory tour during which it becomes familiar with its surroundings and its companions.

From the first months of life, orangutans test out their acrobatic skills.

laborious and discreet; orangutans meet in the trees where short-lived couples are formed for a few days at a time while the female is in her receptive period. Even during their amorous adventures, however, female and male orangutans never 'set up home' together.

The school of life

Gestation in the great apes takes approximately eight months and mothers can give birth roughly every three or four years, at any

The bond of complicity between a young chimpanzee and its mother is key: in fact, if they are reared alone chimpanzees are incapable of communicating with others or of mating.

season. At birth the nursing infant is tiny and very delicate. It is the main focus of interest for an attentive mother. Later, up to the age of two, the young ape alternates between riding around on its mother's back and making careful forays of exploration out into the surrounding world. Play takes up every moment from earliest infancy and is an integral part of the bond between the female ape and her young whom she will care for and bring up for several years. The mother will also protect her young from the sudden moods of a father who is

Chimpanzees are wild about fruit of every kind, especially bananas...

These young chimpanzees are going 'fishing' for termites. They poke a twig into the insect colony and use it to root out these shell-clad delicacies.

The forests of South-East Asia ring with the strange cries uttered by the gibbons and the siamangs. These small tailless apes are the only ones to walk upright on their hind legs almost all the time, and people have long wondered about the family ties linking them to humans. However, the findings of comparative anatomy have distanced them from our branch of the evolutionary tree once and for all. Gibbons are gifted acrobats, and practise gymnastic feats among the trees using their extraordinarily elongated 'super-arms'.

sometimes violent and careless of his own strength. Among gorillas in particular, boisterous play that starts as a game can go tragically wrong.

Ingenious engineering

Thanks to a long apprenticeship lost in the mists of time, chimpanzees are the most skilled of all the animals at using 'tools'. They will rake the ground with a stick, for example, to get hold of a nut lying out of their reach. They will use a stone as a hammer and a hard flat surface as an anvil in order to break open the shell of a nut. Chimpanzees also know how to use a branch as a lever. They will make themselves 'forks' out of sharpened plant stems stripped of their leaves and use these to poke into anthills to catch insects. When very thirsty, they will use leaves as if they were 'spoons'. This animal has many other strings to its bow. In self-defence it will seize a branch and use it as a spear, or throw a stone as a weapon. Chimpanzees also use leaves as umbrellas, as fly-swats or as toilet paper if suffering from persistent diarrhoea. As for twigs, these make good toothpicks and excellent cotton-buds.

This thirsty chimpanzee is using leaves as a drinking vessel.

The proboscis monkey is very difficult to track down in the dense Borneo jungle. With its pensive, solemn pose, this one is reminiscent of a Rodin sculpture.

Old World monkeys

The monkeys of the Old World – Africa and Eurasia – such as baboons, macaques and other cercopithecids have evolved differently from the other apes and monkeys of the planet. Their wide geographical distribution is the result of a conquest hindered only by climate and continental drift.

A seasoned mountaineer, the gelada lives among the heights of Ethiopia. This excellent climber is even capable of clinging on to a wall covered with earthenware tiles.

Baboons are very 'down to earth' but when night falls they climb up into the trees to sleep out of reach of predators. A troop of baboons can number up to several hundred.

The slightest yawn reveals the baboon's incredible array of teeth.

All the Old World apes and monkeys are catarrhine: having a nose with forward-pointing nostrils set close together. They are also the only ones to have the gluteal callosities which set them apart from all the other apes and monkeys on the planet, and their tails are not prehensile. Finally, as in humans, their jaws have thirty-two teeth... Fairly large in size – the great apes are Old World monkeys too – they have conquered all of Africa and all of Asia.

The baboon: hunter and omnivore

The most widespread monkeys in Africa are the baboons. Their long, sharp canines are highly effective hunting weapons. In their natural habitat (the lowlands, savannah and sparse forests of Africa) troops of baboons will attack even large animals such as gazelles or antelopes. They are also well able to content themselves with fruit and plants, however, and they are rather partial to insects.

The hamadryas baboon boasts a kingly mane and princely stature.

For the gourmet baboon, savannah fare is among the finest in all Africa: for the first course, gazelle on a bed of tender grass, and for dessert all the fruit you could wish for.

A big family is a happy family

At first glance the immense troops of baboons appear really quite chaotic. But nothing could be further from the truth: the males in particular are in charge of defending the troop which advances across the savannah in close formation, with the females and infants in the centre. Baboons spend their time on the ground and walk on all fours without ever going upright. At the slightest sign of danger however (the baboon is the leopard's favourite meal), they take refuge in the trees.

Winner of the prize for the finest mask, the mandrill also displays terrifying jaws.

Baboons in disguise

The king of the baboons, with its flowing mane and bare buttocks, is without contest the hamadryas or sacred baboon of Egypt which can sometimes reach the size of a gorilla. Its close relative the mandrill sports a mask of extraordinary colours. This is not a sign of coquetry but rather a useful attribute in ensuring family cohesion. In fact only the dominant male wears this gaudy make-up, putting his superior status on show for all to see.

A long-haired figure swings through the branches: it is the guereza colobus monkey, recognizable by its black and white hair and plumed tail.

▼ Geladas have their own singular style of dress: they have a thick coat, because these animals live at heights of up to 4000 metres on the high plateaux of Ethiopia, and an area of naked pink skin on the chest which fulfils a function similar to that seen in the mandrill — it turns bright red depending on the gelada's disposition and is a good 'barometer' of its mood. Unlike baboons, these animals are particularly timid and flee at the least sign of danger, uttering strange, almost human cries.

Although certain of its attributes are blue, this little cercopithecid is known as the 'green monkey'. In this vast family of monkeys the colouring of the coat can vary enormously.

 ## And thereby hangs a tail...

These monkeys are essentially arboreal and use their long tails as a balancing aid. As their name indicates, the cercopithecids are 'monkeys with tails' – tails which can measure up to 90 centimetres long for a body measuring no more than 70 centimetres. The best known of the cercopithecids is the green monkey, which is renowned for its carefree manner and its curiosity. They are not afraid of playing tricks on other animals, and have been seen sitting astride

This orange-haired white-bearded cercopithecid lives around Brazzaville.

The mandrill's extravagant make-up is highly visible in the virgin forest. Unlike other primates, this large baboon shows its teeth as a sign of friendly greeting.

A close relative of the mandrill, the drill is another large baboon that lives in the African jungle. More discreet in appearance, its black face is encircled by a line of greying beard.

gazelles or toying with an elephant's trunk...

Monkeys marred by nature

The colobus and guereza monkeys belong to the same impaired family – both lack one digit on each hand. In fact their generic name, Colobus, means 'mutilated' in Latin. These large monkeys have extraordinary crowns and coats of long fur, most commonly black and white. Of all the colobus monkeys, the guerezas rule the skies – they can glide through the air by spreading out their arms and legs.

The black mangabey has a curious tuft of hair on the top of its head.

The diana monkey is unreservedly arboreal and never comes down on to the ground. It finds all its food among the treetops.

The great macaque family

Of all the macaque family, only the Barbary ape flourishes both in North Africa and Gibraltar, making it the only monkey living in the wild in Europe. All the other macaques are natives of Asia. Macaques spend most of their time on the ground, but make shelters for themselves in the rocks. The Japanese macaques take the prize for endurance: they live in extraordinary climatic conditions with temperatures of –5°C and a

The wanderoo or liontail macaque sports a square-cut cleopatra-style hairstyle.

The Barbary ape mounts guard over the 'pillars of Hercules'; it lives on both sides of the Straits of Gibraltar. Like the great apes, this macaque is tailless.

This monkey with its corkscrew tail is known as the 'pigtail macaque'. Weighing in at 13 kilograms this is the biggest of the macaques.

metre and a half of snow. They are the most northerly-based monkeys anywhere in the world. Less of an extremist, the wanderoo or liontail macaque lives in the dense and mountainous forests of south-western India. It boasts a helmet of fur and its tail ends in a striking tuft of hair – enough to make the pigtail macaque, the largest of the macaques, quite jealous. Unlike other monkeys which chatter their greetings to one another, the pigtail macaque lifts its head, raises its eyebrows and ogles its partner's nose in a

The entellus enjoys not transcendental, but intestinal meditation.

deliberate fashion by way of greeting.

The entellus at prayer

The entellus or hanuman langur is very widespread in India, where it is often to be found frequenting town centres and temples. It seems to wear a borrowed air of wisdom, as it sits taking in the sun's beneficial rays at sunrise and sunset in a grave and solemn pose as if at prayer... The entellus spends a great deal of the day seated, as it lives exclusively on leaves and needs to rest in order to digest the cellulose it consumes.

Rock-climbing is a sport much enjoyed by the Indian entellus.

The biggest nose in the forest of Borneo

A member of the same family as the entellus, the gentle 'nose-ape' or proboscis monkey is shy and fearful and prefers to confine itself to the steep forest slopes of Asia. The proboscis monkey is endowed with inimitable features: the females and young have a little snub nose, but with increasing age the male's nose becomes truly monstrous. The appendage of an old male proboscis monkey is so enormous that he has to hold it out of the way in order to eat.

The proboscis monkey's nose amplifies its cries of love. When in the mood to serenade, the male utters a sonorous 'honk' not unlike the sound of an old car horn.

While taking the waters at her favourite spa one day, a Japanese female macaque started washing her potatoes before eating them — something no other macaque had ever done before. A few months later, a dozen or so young macaques were doing the same. The adults still seemed reluctant to take to such novel behaviour. Ten years later, the whole community had adopted the technique and even washed their potatoes in sea-water, perhaps in order to enjoy them slightly salted.

The howler monkeys, the serenaders of the forest, are without doubt the noisiest animals in the Amazon jungle.

New World monkeys

The monkeys of the American continent have a markedly less developed brain than their African and Asian cousins. All of the species are arboreal. Most New World monkeys also have a prehensile tail, which they use like a fifth limb as they move through the trees.

It may be musically adept, but the howler monkey cuts a pretty sorry figure as an acrobat, with its slow and extremely cautious movements.

The New World monkeys are platyrrhinians: their noses have widely separated nostrils. They also have four more teeth than humans and than all their Old World cousins. They are of modest size and are to be found mainly in the Amazon forests although some live in Central America. All the American monkeys love hot, moist conditions and they are concentrated exclusively in the tropical zone

Miniature monkeys

Fluffy little creatures with colourful silky fur, marmosets and tamarins are monkeys on a miniature scale. The pygmy marmoset is the smallest of all the monkeys – it measures only 16 centimetres – and its tail is usually longer than the rest of its body. At birth the young of the pygmy marmoset are barely bigger than a broad bean! The marmoset's ears are tipped with a tuft of long hair shaped like the tip of a paintbrush. Tamarins are distinguished from marmosets by their slightly larger size and their talent for jumping. The golden lion tamarins are undoubtedly the strangest of them all. They have a broad red or yellow mane with a metallic glint, similar to that of the lion. The

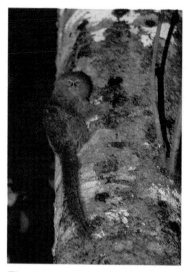

The pygmy marmoset of the Amazon is the 'Tom Thumb' of the monkey world.

The ears of the Geoffroy's tamarin are adorned with black quiffs which it shakes to intimidate its rivals.

These little imps spend their time leaping from branch to branch in the jungles of Colombia. This is the crested tamarin, also nicknamed the 'cotton-top' monkey because of its crown of white fur. When disturbed, this little animal frowns gravely, knitting its brows so that a roll of flesh forms on its forehead. Then it bristles its mane, casts a piercing glance at its adversary — and attacks. Like all the other tamarins the crested tamarins are carnivores, and devour mice and birds with their sharply pointed little teeth.

The proud displays of the magnificent and distinguished emperor tamarin can only be seen in a very restricted area in the south-west of Brazil.

The face of the Goeldi's marmoset is similar to that of a Yorkshire terrier.

emperor tamarin of the Amazon forest is certainly the most delightful. This extremely rare little monkey has a moustache of very long whiskers worthy of any Chinese emperor. The Goeldi's marmoset, which is not in fact a true tamarin at all, a tiny, all-black monkey, is the sole representative of the genus Callimico which translates literally as 'beautiful little monkey'.

A spider a metre across

Ateles or spider monkeys use their extraordinarily

powerful tails to grasp branches and swing and somersault through the trees. Spider monkeys also use their tails to grasp objects. The woolly monkey or lagothrix has the same general build as the spider monkey. Its coat is so thick that it seems dressed to spend the winter in a harsher climate.

All set and ready for the fashion show

Howler monkeys announce their presence and the extent of their

The spider monkey uses its four limbs as much as its tail.

Related to the spider monkey, the woolly monkey is the unrivalled champion in acrobatics. It thinks nothing of letting itself drop from a height of 10 metres.

'Ah-oo, ah-oo, ah-oo...': this strange cry ringing through the forests of Guatemala is the resonant call-sign of the howler monkey.

The white-faced saki wears a perfect Pierrot mask.

territory by voicing powerful cries that can carry over distances of 5 kilometres. These howls serve to drive back their neighbours, the capuchin monkeys which are found throughout the forests of South America. Other more unusual monkeys inhabit the banks of the Amazon: the sakis and the uakaris. Their fur is so long that it gives a false impression of the size of their bodies. The monk saki, white faced saki and capuchin saki all look as if they had just come from

Anchored to the branches by their prehensile tails, red howler monkeys move comfortably through the Amazon jungle's cathedral of greenery.

This little woolly monkey jealously guards the fruit in which it delights. These animals have an insatiable appetite out of all proportion to their size.

When the red uakari displays its face, the green setting of the Amazon forest seems for all the world like the backdrop for a ghost train.

a fashion show; the only lapse in good taste is committed by the red uakari which, with its bald red head, looks as if it had suffered serious burns.

The 'stop-out'

As day draws to a close, monkeys retire for the night. Only the night monkey opens its great eyes in the darkness and sets out hunting. This preference for the nocturnal life is a primitive trait, also found in the monkey's cousins the prosimians.

Owl-like eyes allow the night monkey to lead the life of a real night-owl.

The startled eyes of the lesser bushbaby, whose plangent little cries are strangely reminiscent of those of human babies.

Primates and their relatives

The vast family of primates is not confined to apes and monkeys alone. Their cousins the lemurs, bushbabies and lorises have taken different evolutionary paths – though not always with the same success. In fact most of them are now under threat of disapearing.

The thrust and spring achieved by the black lemur would leave the greatest athletes behind: this lemur is barely a metre tall but can leap a distance of more than 8 metres.

T he ancestor of all primates, which may have resembled today's tree shrew, was a small insect-eating animal that lived some 100 million years ago. It first adapted gradually to an arboreal life. In order to see well among the trees its eyes grew larger and moved towards the front of the face giving excellent vision in three dimensions. In order to move better through this new universe, the thumb and big toe 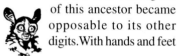 of this ancestor became opposable to its other digits. With hands and feet

Our early ancestors looked something like this tree shrew with its strange ears.

The process of natural selection got the better of Neanderthal man, who disappeared mysteriously 50,000 years ago. Homo sapiens (humans) have been luckier.

Mouse lemurs move around using their hands and feet, equipped with opposable thumbs, to grasp the branches. A small step for them but a great leap for mankind.

Female bonobos have nothing to envy our earliest grandmothers.

transformed into 'pincers', our distant ancestor's life underwent a radical change: from now on it could grasp the branches that grew all around it. It became very proficient at this and no longer had any use for its claws which turned into nails. Its brain grew larger and accommodated the new cerebral structures needed to cope with a complex environment. The way was open to the evolution of apes and monkeys (simians) and humans, as well as lemurs, lorises, bushbabies and tree shrews (prosimians).

The lesser mouse lemur is without contest the smallest of all the primates and in fact looks more like a hamster. It measures only 12 centimetres and weighs barely 50 grams.

The last direct representative of the ancestor of all primates — including humankind — is the tree shrew, which has survived to the present day and offers a 'living model' of our own past. At first sight it is hard to imagine that this strange squirrel could be the closest living descendant of our forebears. In fact these curious creatures have no more than a few cranial bones to show that they belong to the line that gave rise to the apes, monkeys and humans...

Madagascar, last refuge of the lemur family

The mother indris bounds along carrying her young like a rucksack.

Like furry, rather touching ghosts, active mainly at night, the lemurs haunt the forests of Madagascar uttering strange sorrowful cries. Many lemurs have enormous red-brown eyes adapted to night vision but do not perceive colours. The last lemurs on the planet live in Madagascar which is home to examples of every shape and size. The mouse lemur is a Lilliputian among lemurs. Their tiny cries are so high-pitched that the human ear can barely hear them. Though much bigger, the hapalemurs and other lepilemurs are much less lively and sleep all day, but when night has fallen they career through the treetops performing extraordinary acrobatic feats.

The lemur – a 'genuine imitation' monkey

The lemurs bear a much greater resemblance to the typical monkey. They are highly social animals, and use a whole range of howls and grimaces to ensure the cohesion of their group. The males have a gland on the shoulder which allows them to mark a vast expanse of territory. Lemurs have extremely colourful

coats, with a strange pair of spectacles on the face and a series of 14 white rings on the tail which mark them as belonging to the catta species. As for the other lemurs (the crowned lemur, the black and white ruffed lemur, the black lemur...), rich costume is still in fashion at the lemur family carnival. The indris, the largest of them all, serves as a reminder that before the human race arrived in Madagascar there were members of the lemur family in existence that were bigger than gorillas.

The lepilemur is not afraid to rub against even the sharpest thorns.

Lemurs are positively obsessed with cleanliness. They all have a large claw on the second toe which they use to comb their fur with meticulous care.

The aye-aye of Madagascar only makes the briefest of appearances these days: its living space is so severely depleted that its survival is threatened.

Sitting in the lotus position, the indris takes its daily sun-bath. It basks in the sun's rays like this every morning, and does not become active until the hottest hours of the day.

Champion gliders, the indris improve their range thanks to a parachute-like membrane connecting their limbs to their body.

Forgotten by the world

Only a few other prosimians are to be found anywhere else on the planet: the lorises of Central Africa, India and South-East Asia, the bushbabies of Africa and the tarsiers of the Philippines. The slender loris (India) has owl-like eyes and its limbs are so long that one would think it walked on stilts. It is a slow and clumsy animal. Lazier still, the slow loris (Indonesia) is a completely apathetic ball of fur. The bushbabies of Senegal, on the other hand, are lively and

Birds of a feather flock together? Not in the case of the black lemur couples.

expert jumpers. The unrivalled gymnastics champion, however, is still the tarsier of the Philippines, whose slender and elongated fingers and toes enables it to leap like a frog. To add to the strangeness of this animal, each of its great eyes is almost larger than its brain. The prosimians – literally 'pre-monkeys' – do not have the intellectual capacities of their more highly evolved cousins.

The apes, close relatives of humans

Pygmy chimpanzees bear a striking physical and behavioural resemblance to humans. This is hardly surprising, since they share 99 percent of their genetic inheritance with us. Analysing blood samples from the great apes has made it possible to date the moment at which the different lines diverged: the lineage of the orangutan appears to have separated from the human line over 14 million years ago, that of the gorilla 9 to 6 million years ago and that of the chimpanzee only 7 to 5 million years ago.

On the trail of humans

The birthplace of humanity was probably Africa: this is where most fossils of hominids have

The ring-tailed lemur bows sedately before bounding out of sight.

The indris are the biggest members of the lemur family and measure almost a metre long. During the hot season they like to stretch out comfortably along the branches.

With its rodent's incisors and its bat-like ears, the aye-aye is without a doubt the most extraordinary animal in the forests of Madagascar, and long escaped classification. This creature of the night has an inordinately large middle finger which it uses to eat: the aye-aye probes the worm-eaten branches by striking them with its long fingers and tracks down the insects and larvae sheltering under the bark. During the day it takes shelter in its nest, a round ball of leaves and bits of branch hanging in the treetops.

When a person meets the bonobo's profound gaze it is as if they were looking into a 'mirror from the past'.

The most senior member of humankind is Lucy, an Australopithecus afarensis discovered in 1974 in Ethiopia. About 5 million years ago, Lucy was a slender young woman a little over a metre tall. She already walked upright, but would climb into the trees in the event of danger. Her arms were long, her eyebrow arches pronounced and her jaws thrust forward. She and her cousin Ramidus, who lived at approximately the same time, comprise the first known links to a humanity still in its infancy.

It is a sign of bad luck in the Philippines to cross a tarsier's path.

been discovered and it is also the homeland of chimpanzees and the gorillas. The oldest human remains were found to the east of the Great Rift Valley in Ethiopia, an immense fault which has split the African continent apart for over ten million years. West of the Great Rift Valley lie the bones of the great apes.

East Side Story

This distribution is the origin of the 'East Side Story' hypothesis. The mountain chain which arose as a result of the opening up of the Rift would have caused a significant reduction in rainfall in the east of Africa. Most of the great apes found refuge in the forests of the west, which still enjoyed a wet climate. Some, however, remained on the eastern side of the barrier, and were forced to adapt to the drought. As the trees gradually disappeared, these 'pre-humans' came down on to the ground and changed their diet, becoming omnivores. Later, the need to stand upright and walk on two feet in order to survive in a hostile savannah freed their hands – a prelude to the making of weapons and tools. A few million years later, this ancestor has turned into *Homo sapiens*, invaded the world and ventured into space.

Part two

Monkeys in Our World

Apes and monkeys are particularly highly venerated in Asia. The Hindu monkey-god Hanuman is always represented surrounded by lotus flowers and clouds of incense.

Monkeys as living gods

Great civilizations have lent the apes and monkeys innumerable virtues: wisdom, spirituality, omniscience... Respected and venerated, the monkey can rise from the rank of beast to that of a living god.

Low-reliefs depicting the monkey people in the temple of Borobadur, on the island of Java. This cosmically symbolic temple, dating from 850 AD, traces the life of the Buddha.

In the Balinese barong dance-drama, which represents the battle between the forces of good and evil, the mischievous, mocking monkey constantly defies the Barong lion.

Those who are in search of something mystical may often draw their inspiration from the postures, grimaces and antics of an animal. The creature then becomes a spiritual reference-point – and the apes and monkeys, having such a human look and bearing, have always been an animal of choice in this respect.

The two-headed god Thoth

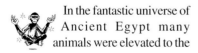 In the fantastic universe of Ancient Egypt many animals were elevated to the

Blue monkeys adorn the ancient ruins on the Aegean islands and Crete.

rank of deity, and the monkey came to occupy one of the foremost places in this animal pantheon. The hamadryas baboon in particular, with its royal mane and its solemn air, seems naturally imbued with spirituality. So it was that in Hermopolis – a religious centre of great importance in Ancient Egypt – the god Thoth could have two faces: he was represented in turn with the head of an ibis or the head of a hamadryas baboon. The Egyptians considered this monkey as a lunar animal, as the

The Minoans attributed mythical powers to apes and monkeys as early as 3000 BC.

In Ancient Egypt, and especially the city of Hermopolis, the cult-centre of the god Thoth situated 300 kilometres south of Cairo, baboons were the masters of learning and time.

females' menstrual cycle is synchronized with the cycles of that astral body of the night. The moon was then the unit of measurement of time. So Thoth and his monkey-like face symbolized reckoning and the mind. He was invoked whenever an intellectual solution was sought to a problem set, and Thoth was very soon regarded as the god of universal learning, inventor of the sciences, the arts, language and writing. This 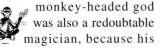 monkey-headed god was also a redoubtable magician, because his

Mummies attest to the venerated status of baboons in Ancient Egypt.

Dozens of baboons watched over the mummy of the pharaoh Tutankhamun. The baboon-god Thoth accompanied the pharaohs on their journey into the Hereafter.

The baboon-god Thoth, the god of writing and knowledge, was often represented as an elegantly dressed cynocephalus who stood alongside Egypt's greatest pharaohs.

mastery of words allowed him to formulate incantations. In addition to this, in Egyptian mythology baboons took part in the weighing of souls before they set out on their final journey to the kingdom of the dead. They have been found depicted in the tombs of pharaohs and dignitaries such as Tutankhamun and Rekhmire'.

The baboon cult

Venerated, respected and feared by all, the baboons greeting the dawning of each new day with

The pharaohs' royal scribes were believed to be inspired by baboons.

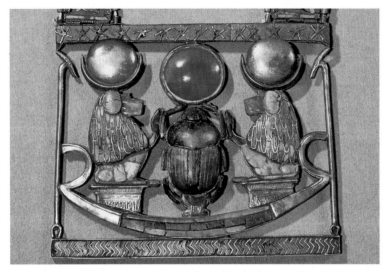

A piece of Egyptian jewellery with a scarab flanked by two baboons. The scarab, associated with the rising of the sun, was the idol of the sacred baboons.

A huge statue of a baboon dominated the centre of the ancient city of Hermopolis.

their piercing cries were considered to be worshipping the sun. So it was that the Egyptians often depicted them with their arms raised, deep in fervent prayer. Large numbers of the faithful would come to the temples of Hermopolis to bring them offerings, generally food and wine, in order to win their protection.

The companion baboon

As living gods the baboons had inestimable value, and they were

The Ancient Egyptians believed that the Hamadryas baboons worshipped the sun. Every morning, they celebrated the sunrise by raising their hands towards the 'diurnal star'.

often given as ceremonial gifts to dignitaries of the highest rank who could thus walk their iconic fetish on a leash. Just like the most powerful pharaohs, baboons were mummified in a sitting position when they died and whole necropolises were devoted to them.

The sacred monkey of India

The entellus or hanuman langur is an object of veneration in the Indies to this day. The posture of these animals sitting 'at prayer' expresses such wisdom that every Hindu is reminded that they are among the heroes of that great epic, the *Ramayana*. This saga recounts the life of prince Rama, living incarnation of the god Vishnu. When Rama's wife is kidnapped by the wicked and lecherous giant Ravana, the monkey people are offended by such ill-mannered behaviour and decide to come to the prince's assistance. Sugriva the monkey king and his minister the mischievous Hanuman lead an expedition into the giant's gardens to deliver the unhappy captive. The operation is a success. But Hanuman's greediness does him an ill turn in the end when, bringing up the rear he lingers in the giant's gardens

The entellus monkey leads a peaceful existence in Hindu temples.

Entellus monkeys enjoy sacred status in India where these much venerated creatures are given the freedom of the cities. So much so that they breed like rabbits...

In China and throughout South-East Asia a popular story, 'Journey to West', which recounts the long journey of the Monkey King who sets out for the west in search of the sacred texts of Buddhism. Based on the pilgrimage of Xuan Zang, this state is understood to represent the allegorical clash of Taoism with the then nascent religion of Buddhism. During the 1970s it was adapted in the form of a cartoon, using a brave little monkey to bring the foundations of this religion to a youthful audience.

Indian sadhus take a vow of chastity and silence in order to devote themselves entirely to a life of meditation. Baboons are the constant companions of these wandering holy men.

and is caught red-handed stealing mangoes. The sentence is given without appeal: Hanuman must be put to death by fire. He manages to escape the pyre and give his executioners the slip, but alas his hands and face are burned and all his descendants still bear the marks of his terrible ordeal: all entellus monkeys have black hands and faces.

An everyday deity

Like the sacred cows, the entellus enjoys a privileged status in Indian society. It is the focus of a

The monkeys were among the heroes of that great Hindu epic, the *Ramayana*.

cult in Hindu temples and even its skeleton is an object of veneration. They are also often to be seen in town centres wandering about with perfect impunity, and have become so accustomed to city life that they have largely given up their arboreal habits.

A powerful symbol

In India the statue of the monkey-god Hanuman is a source of fertility. Infertile women take off their clothes and worship the

Entellus monkeys enjoy a plentiful supply of food offerings.

In South-East Asia, monkeys are central to the Buddhist and Taoist religions. In fact, the Jade Emperor took a great liking to the 'thief of the peaches of immortality'.

This miniature from Rajasthan depicts the epic journey of prince Rama. Every Hindu learns about his successful collaboration with the monkey people.

▼ Chinese astrology based on the lunar calendar was established in the sixth century AD. It has 12 signs represented by the 12 animals which, according to legend, responded to the appeal of the Jade Emperor. People born in 1944, 1956, 1980 and 1992 belong to the sign of the monkey. They are intelligent, and good at influencing others but also tend to be over-enthusiastic, easily discouraged and confused... Monkeys are compatible with dragons and with rats but not with tigers.

In Chinese calligraphy, the character for monkey is rich in associations.

香港 HONG KONG

ne Monkey 1992

effigy in suggestive positions, thus recovering their fertility completely. The name of Hanuman written on gold leaf can help with a difficult childbirth. In Thailand a tattoo of the monkey-god Hanuman is a magical symbol of strength and invincibility for men.

The good-luck monkey of the Japanese

The Japanese are one of many civilizations that have placed monkeys on a pedestal. Woven or painted icons depicting good-luck monkeys are found hanging in many Japanese households. The Japanese have a profound respect for this animal and a particular regard for their own macaques which brave the rigours of winter especially on the island of Yakishima. Macaques play a vital role in Japanese mythology, literature and art. There is even a deified monkey, Sarutahiko, which is celebrated each year throughout the Japanese archipelago with lively parades and festivals. And finally, the Japanese macaque is found throughout in Buddhist Asia. Three of them represent one of the Buddhist principles of discretion: 'see no evil, hear no evil, speak no evil'.

The western world's love-affair with its pets sometimes has religious connotations. This monkey in Los Angeles has just undergone an elaborate christening ceremony.

The temple of Yogyakarta on the island of Java is decorated with stylised monkeys.

The sidereal monkey of the Pre-Colombian civilizations

The ancient Aztecs and Mayas associated the monkey with the sun-god, god of song and music but also prince of flowers. The monkey is also one of the powerful signs in the Aztec calendar. People born under this sign will be respected artisans or artists despite an ardent sexual temperament going beyond the bounds of the forbidden. In this part of the world, though, representation of the

The huge monkey traced on the Nazca plateau of southern Peru is like something out of science-fiction. Created by a pre-Incan civilisation, it is only visible from the air.

monkey can take more disconcerting turns. On the Nazca plateau in Southern Peru, a civilization dating from before the Incas traced extraordinary drawings on the ground. Among these gigantic figures is a monkey over 100 metres across, visible from the sky. The exact role of this image dating from 300 AD remains unexplained. Celestial calendar, sacred site of worship, a sports ground or a landing-site for UFOs... one theory is as good as another, and the site remains a mystery.

For pre-Columbian cultures, the monkey was closely associated with the sun-god.

The 'Jocko' (chimpanzee) drawn by the French encyclopaedist Buffon (1707-88) reflects the anthropomorphic approach of 18th-century European naturalists.

The missing link

Distant cousin or close relative, the links in the line of descent between monkeys and humans are beyond doubt. Before the theory of evolution was accepted by scientists, however, drawing parallels between animals and humans was sometimes considered unacceptable.

In 1974, the paleontologist Yves Coppens discovered the remains of the hominid that became popularly known as Lucy.

The resemblance between humans and the apes and monkeys has fascinated every culture on the planet and for many there is an obvious link of kinship between the two.

Degenerate humans

In the culture of a large number of peoples in Africa and Asia, for example, apes and monkeys are regarded as lazy humans. On the island of Borneo it is said that the orangutan (whose name means 'man of the forest' in Malay) actually has the

In Borneo, orangutans are considered to be lazy human beings.

This miniature King Kong has fired the human imagination for over four centuries. Early descriptions of gorillas and chimpanzees refer to 'strange men'.

Humans and chimpanzees are the only items not on the menu of the Twa Pygmies. According to an ancestral proverb, monkeys were once their ancestors.

power of speech but avoids revealing the fact for fear of being made to work. According to the mythology of the Dyaks – one of the peoples of Indonesia – when the bird gods who created the world made the monkeys they wanted to remake humans but got the recipe wrong.

A simian-like Adam

The Christian religions too mix human and simian together in certain versions of the creation of the world. In the 17th century, for

Early western explorers tended to confuse pygmies and chimpanzees.

From Aesop to the *Fables* of La Fontaine (1621-95), classical writers have presented the monkey as a cunning creature who uses his human appearance to trick other animals.

The Dutch physician Jacob Bontius was one of the first to observe orangutans in 1630. He was clearly enchanted by them: 'the female appears modest,' he relates, 'covering herself with her hands at the sight of unfamiliar male persons; able to cry, moan and accomplish all the other acts of man so that nothing would seem to be wanting but speech'. During the 19th century, transformist theories made the orangutan the darling of the European zoos. Sadly most died of tuberculosis.

According to some Biblical tales from Eastern Europe, Adam had a monkey's tail.

example, it was thought that at the time of Genesis God had made man out of a piece of clay. With the rest of the clay, the Creator made the much more slightly-built form of woman. Not knowing what to do with the material left over, he created miniature people – the pygmies and the apes and monkeys. In certain tales from Eastern Europe Adam even had a tail – a strange detail for a being created in the image of his God.

Evolution in reverse

For the natives of North America, where monkeys disappeared several thousand years ago, humankind really does descend from the apes and is really no more than a coarse by-product of monkey-kind. In fact at the beginning of the world humans were hairy and endowed with a tail. The brash unconcern of these impudent creatures incurred the wrath of the great Manitou who punished men by depriving them of their posterior appendage with which, according to legend, he made woman.

Mistaken by identity

Before the process of determining the species was completely

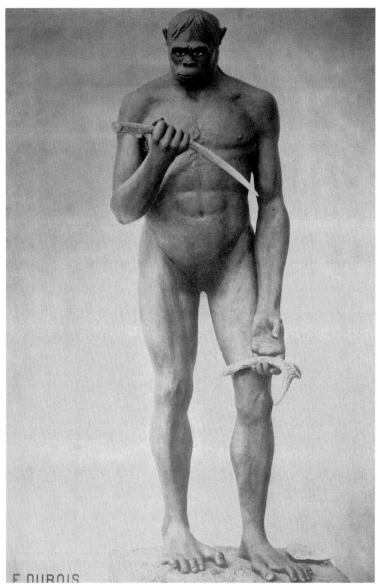

F. DUBOIS

In 1891, the Dutch physician Eugene Dubois discovered the remains of 'Java man' alias *Pithecanthropus* (from the Greek *pithêkos* = ape and *anthrôpos* = man).

established, the discovery of the great anthropoid apes by western explorers gave free rein to every kind of fantasy and to terrible errors. At the time of the great discoveries of the 16th century, accounts brought back from Africa offered a jumble of descriptions mixing up not only the evil chimpanzee and the monstrous gorilla but also albino Africans and the Pygmies. Disturbingly, members of all of these species were captured, and stuffed by taxidermists for the greater glory of Science.

At the dawn of humanity, *Australopithecus* (from the Greek *austrâlis* = southern and *pithêkos* = ape) emerged from the darkness of time.

It took over a century, from the discovery of the first hominoid fossils (1856) to the discovery of Lucy, to establish the connection between apes and human beings.

In many civilisations, the ape played a key role in the myth of the Creation. For some, it was the ape that evolved from humans.

Knowing the secret of fire, *Homo sapiens* moved away from his simian ancestry.

The man-monkey relationship

The nature of the monkey was a subject of great debate. Aristotle, for example, writing 22 centuries before the theory of evolution, mentions the human features of animals resembling the baboon or the Barbary ape. Starting at the time of the Enlightenment, a bitter argument concerning the relationship linking humans and apes developed between the scientists and the guardians of faith in the Western world. At this time Carolus Linnaeus (1707–1778),

the inventor of the modern system of classification, grouped humans and monkeys together in the same group: the primates. Later, in 1809, the father of transformism Lamarck was the first to refer to a progressive change from monkey to human. When the English scholar Darwin (1809–1882) confirmed this hypothesis and developed his theory of evolution in 1860 it was all too much for the Church, which from then on categorically rejected the idea that a single atom of kinship could possibly exist between its faithful flock and the savage beast.

Charles Darwin's (1809-82) *Theory of Evolution* was widely caricatured.

Today, our origins are traced and explained in museums and educational books. However, a few tenacious Creationists still refuse to accept the theory of evolution.

Irrefutable proof

During the course of the 19th century, the discovery of the first fossils of hominids – Cro-Magnon man and Neanderthal man – brought irrefutable proof of the simian origins of humans. It still remained to find and clearly identify the link that joined humans and apes together. In 1891, the discovery of pithecanthropus or 'Java man' offered an initial answer to this question and situated the birthplace of humanity in Asia. In the light of the latest fossils exhumed since 1925, however, the scientific community as a whole is in agreement that the human species emerged in Africa. The link between the australopithecines and the apes is still missing...

The Yeti or Abominable Snowman roams the mountains of the Himalayas.

Yeti and company

The wildest hopes continue to go around regarding the real existence of anthropoids as yet unknown. The Yeti of the Himalayas is one of the most celebrated examples, but the Yiren of China, Zania on the shores of the Black Sea, the Kaptars and Almasti of Russia and the American Bigfoot are as sought after as their Himalayan cousin...

Several generations of Americans have taken the Bigfoot to their hearts. In the film *Bigfoot and the Andersons*, a tender-hearted anthropoid is adopted by an ordinary family.

The American Bigfoot or sasquatch is the object of some controversy: picture-chasers argue over the Internet about the authenticity of blurred or visibly faked photographs: footprints, a hairy silhouette in the woods, even the genetic analysis of hairs. To this day no expert worthy of the name has been able to verify the truth of the collected 'evidence'. But the impassioned fans of cryptozoology have already classified it in a new genus — gigantopithecus — and wonder about its relationship with Neanderthal man.

Journal des Voyage

JOURNAL HEBDOMADAIRE
• 146, Rue Montmartre, PARIS (2ᵉ)

et des Aventures de Terre et de Mer

DANS LA PEAU D'UN SINGE

Grand Roman d'Aventures par G. Le Faure

When it comes to monsters thirsting for blood, apes come a close second to
Frankenstein, Dracula and werewolves as a major box-office attraction.

The battle between brothers

Humans can be infuriated by a meeting with their animal double – finding them stupid, quarrelsome, ugly or machiavellian. The ape, has been variously transformed into a caricature, a rival who has to be wiped out, a sex-fiend or a monster to be put on show in the fairground.

Monkeys are a common source of food in Africa where they are not classified among the primates but regarded as ordinary 'bush meat'.

The shadow of a fiendish monkey hangs over this Tuscan garden. In Europe, the monkey's tormented face is the irrefutable sign of its diabolic nature.

The figure of King Kong is still sowing panic at Universal Studios in Los Angeles.

F or many people the monkey's face, a caricature of their own, is the irrefutable sign of a diabolic nature. The fact of having a hairy coat and a tail completes a picture that smacks of heresy...

Crimes and punishments

The Egyptians who worshipped Thoth, their monkey-god, feared Baba – a lecherous and slavering baboon-devil who stripped the dead of their virility. Another disturbing representation of the monkey appeared in

Baba, the lecherous Egyptian baboon-devil, had no sense of modesty.

Ancient Egypt – the hieroglyph representing anger was invariably followed by a drawing of a baboon showing its teeth. In Greek mythology, the Cercopes were a terrible band of brigands who were transformed into monkeys by Zeus. They gave their name to the cercopithecids of Africa. In Rome, the law used monkeys to administer its punishments: a parricide would be beaten with red rods, then shut in a sack with an ape. This showed criminals that they were no more than the caricature of a

The accounts of early explorers described bloodthirsty animals and black hairy creatures that were part man, part beast.

Roman. Those who built the Tower of Babel, too, were punished for having tried to reach the heavens, as is explained in the Talmud, which goes on to add that these ambitious architects were transformed into monkeys. Most legends of a Biblical nature also make the monkey a representative of evil: a monkey is the companion of the serpent, the tempter that leads Adam and Eve to sin

The devil personified

The Romanesque churches of Medieval Europe overflowed with gargoyles, sculptures and iconography of every kind which depicted the monkey's face as fiendish and tormented. Its provocative buffoonery and its bestial side, associated with a bodily form that was almost human, made the monkey an ideal scapegoat for the Christians. Even the reformer Luther accused them, saying 'I believe that the Devil inhabits monkeys male and female that they might counterfeit humans so well.'

A sign of ill-fortune

For the Amerindians, the Persians, the Egyptians and Westerners alike, to dream of a

Actor Charlton Heston encounters the harsh law of the primates.

The Tower of Babel, built in an attempt to reach heaven, flouted God's supremacy. He punished the pretentious architects by turning them into monkeys.

The film Planet of the Apes (1968) suggests a disturbing version of the evolution of species. Three astronauts hurled into the future find themselves on a strange planet where roles are reversed. Here humans are stupid beasts hunted by monkeys who have taken power: the orangutans are judges and priests, the chimpanzees are scholars and the gorillas are the police. With the help of two chimpanzee archaeologists, Zira and Cornelius, Taylor (Charlton Heston) realises the truth: he has come back to Earth.

The Berbers of North Africa never uttered the word 'monkey' but referred to 'the mountain ones'.

monkey is a bad omen. For a long time the Berbers of North Africa had a taboo against uttering the word 'monkey'. At that time the Barbary apes inhabiting the region were referred to as 'the mountain ones' or 'the almond-lovers'. To drive them away the villagers would catch one, tie a bell around its neck and deck it out in a red waistcoat to frighten off its fellow-apes. In Japan, there is a tradition that the word 'monkey' must never be spoken at a wedding: if it were, the

In spite of official bans and the fact that it is a protected – and endangered – species, gorillas are still widely hunted in Africa for their meat.

Monkeys – regarded as 'crop-eating pests' by African farmers – can decimate a field in only a few days.

terrified bride would inevitably flee the ceremony and run away as fast as her legs would carry her.

Vermin

In much more prosaic fashion, monkeys are regarded as a crop-eating pest in Africa where they are in direct competition with the human population in the search for food. They have always been hunted for this reason. In complete contrast, in Lobpuri in Thailand the macaques are held in such great respect that the

A hunter proudly brandishing his trophy.

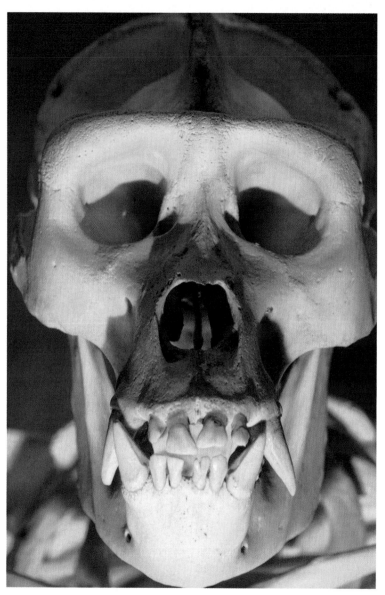

With its pointed teeth, prominent eyebrow arches and projecting lower jaw, the gorilla looks as if it has just stepped off a ghost train.

inhabitants turn a blind eye to all their quirks – and the monkeys have literally taken possession of the city. Shoplifting, sabotage of the communications networks, attacks on private property – the macaque gangs are masters of all they survey.

The 'serial killer'

In 1841, in his *The Murders in the Rue Morgue* , Edgar Allen Poe presented the story of an orangutan which, having escaped from its cage, finds shelter in the

Béla Lugosi in the clutches of the 'serial killer' in *The Murders in the Rue Morgue* .

Although this young orphaned gorilla has lost its freedom, it has perhaps found a safe haven with the humans who have taken it in.

The so-called 'monkey banquet' held in Lobpuri in Thailand tends to turn into something of an orgy. Once they have devoured the offerings, the hungry macaques go on the rampage.

The orangutan Fu Manchu was a true escape artist.

home of Madame L'Espanaye and her daughter. Terrified by the two women's cries of fear, the animal seizes a razor and cuts their throats. This terrible tale was actually inspired by a true story which shows monkeys in an extremely favourable light: Fu Manchu, an orangutan in the zoo of the little town of Omaha in the USA, used to leave its prison every night and calmly shut the door behind it. Inside the cage there was not a single clue to show how this stratagem was achieved. It transpired that

great russet 'Houdini' used to hide a metal shank inside its cheek and use it to pick the locks. Then it would stroll at leisure through the parks of the city without a single complaint ever being made against it.

The fantastic monkey

When the great apes were discovered, the typical fairground freak-shows were enriched by the addition of a new, black and hairy creature – the terrible gorilla or the disturbing chimpanzee. Side

The orangutan used to be put on show as a monster in zoos and fairgrounds.

In Walt Disney's *Lion King*, the mandrill Rafiki disguises himself as a mad magician. He is in fact a wise monkey who advises all the animals and puts the Lion King on the throne.

In 1933, *King Kong* terrorised an entire generation. As well as being fascinated by its special effects, filmgoers were captivated by this tale about a love-sick gorilla.

The fear of a monstrous crossbreed between monkey and human is found in numerous legends. One such was put about by Pope Alexander II in the 11th century. A terrible drama was being lived out in the family of one of his friends, an Italian count, whose wife had deserted him in favour of a vigorous and jealous ape. The fruit of this union was a boy with a simian look, who at the age of 20 had still not mastered speech. The same salacious theme was taken up by many writers, in fantastical or moralistic short stories.

Jessica Lange captures the gorilla's heart in the 1976 remake of *King Kong*.

by side with the limbless man or the bat-child, the monkey-woman took her place in a piece of fairground trickery designed to fool the gullible customer. Circus menageries too liked to display great gorillas, presenting them as the most terrifying creatures in the world.

King Kong

At the beginning of the 1930s the myth of the monstrous ape reached its zenith with King Kong. Torn away from his island, the hairy colossus cannot cope with city life and breaks his chains the better to sow panic throughout New York. Holding the delicate figure of a platinum-blonde music-hall star in one hand, Kong climbs up the Empire State Building at the top of which a squadron of fighter planes are waiting for him. Despite his efforts to swat away this new breed of mosquitoes, the tender-hearted giant is shot down and tumbles from the skyscraper after having carefully set down his sweetheart on a cornice of the building. Apart from the classic theme of Beauty and the Beast, this modern fable presents a conflict between indomitable Nature and a modern USA in the grip of an unprecedented

Monkeys have long had a worldwide reputation as sex maniacs. Because of their human appearance and behaviour, copulation among primates was considered the epitome of shamelessness and lechery.

economic crisis. Some have even seen in the Empire State Building the only phallic symbol capable of measuring up to the scale of the monster.

The sex maniac

Inflamed sexuality, shamelessness and lechery are the characteristics attributed to the apes and monkeys in many civilizations. In Africa as in Asia, there are legends on the theme of the monkey as rapist carrying out

In 1859, Gustave Frémier's *Le Gorille enlevant une négresse* (Gorilla carrying off a Negress) provoked a public outcry.

its wicked deeds in organized bands or alone. The priapic animal sets itself up as a rival and defies the faltering virility of men. In the tales of the *Thousand and One Nights*, the impotent butcher Wardan appeals to a sorceress to reawaken his former ardour. He means to tear the Vizier's daughter – a renowned nymphomaniac – away from the claws of an enormous ape with which she spends all her nights because, according to the tale, 'there is none more prolific in onset than the monkey'.

When human beings descend into Hell, their true nature is revealed.

The bawdy monkey was a popular figure with cartoonists and often replaced the lover in the 'eternal triangle' of popular farce.

Given their agility and love of pulling faces, monkeys make natural entertainers, particularly when it comes to juggling and slapstick.

Man's best friend

Whether as public entertainer, companion in good fortune or bad, scholar or guinea-pig, the monkey has always had a place in human society. Sometimes the artist, sometimes the source of inspiration, its image has evolved over the course of the centuries.

Macaques are trained to give farmers a helping hand in return for a few titbits. There are 'training schools' for monkeys in countries all over the world.

Monkeys are also trained to help quadriplegics. They perform extremely precise movements with great delicacy and devotion.

Some fruitful associations can be created when people decide to make the monkey part of their everyday lives, even if it's usually the humans who get the most benefit out of the situation. Monkeys and humans can become friends, or at least genuine partners.

The monkey-clown

At the circus, in the zoo, in cinema or in advertising, monkeys are the delight of their human audience. With their range of facial expressions,

As public entertainers, monkeys are paid peanuts.

they are often linked in the West with clowns and buffoons – from the royal courts of yesteryear to the shows and performances of today. At one time, entertainers with monkeys were so much appreciated that they were entitled to exemption from paying tolls when they crossed toll bridges: 'monkey business' was the coin they paid in.

The strength of Gibraltar

A little bit of the stability of the British Empire rests on the

The monkey's artistic talents were already being put to the test in the 17th century.

Today, chimpanzees are still regarded as public entertainers. Their widespread use in advertising is the ultimate attribution of human form and behaviour.

shoulders of the Barbary ape. According to tradition, the day the Barbary apes disappear from the Rock the British army will have to abandon the scene. They are especially pampered for this reason, and during World War II Sir Winston Churchill even boosted their numbers so as to be sure of keeping control of the straits.

Combining business with pleasure

Monkeys, particularly marmosets and capuchins, are highly prized as pets. During the 18th century they readily took the place of the traditional parrot on the shoulder of the Caribbean pirates. In Africa and particularly in Asia the local monkeys, such as the green monkey or the incredible proboscis monkey, have also been tamed and kept for generations. Women even breastfeed infant animals. Thanks to their capacity to learn, some have been trained to help humans in their work. In Egypt monkeys took part in fruit-picking; in Arabia they were trained to act as guard-monkeys – but also in the art of divesting passers-by of their belongings. On another note, with their talent for water-divining the chacma baboons of South Africa help

The famous Barbary apes have become the symbol of Gibraltar.

Tarzan the ape man, earl of Greystoke and lord of the jungle, was created in 1912 by US novelist Edgar Rice Burroughs. Among hundreds of versions on the big and the small screen, in cartoons and in CD-ROMs, the most famous are those featuring the former swimming champion Johnny Weismuller. Brought up among the apes, Tarzan is at one with nature and shares his adventures with the faithful female chimpanzee Cheeta. He knows how to talk to the animals, but he knows how to talk to women too: 'Me Tarzan, you Jane...'

From roller skating and skiing to hang gliding and sub-aqua diving, monkeys are the – often unwilling – participants in a wide range of different sports.

Monkeys have been taught to communicate with sign language and ideograms.

people find phreatic water layers. The pigtail macaques in Malaysia are still trained to climb up into the coconut palms and pull down the ripe coconuts. Only the females and juveniles enjoy this privilege as the males are considered too dangerous.

A laboratory animal

The monkey is also a vital 'partner' in scientific research. Its anatomical and behavioural similarities to humans have made

A vital 'partner' in medical and scientific research.

it a good experimental model despite the protests of the animal protection leagues. The rhesus macaque has given its name to a blood factor, and the first representative of the US to go into space was a female monkey. Today, the first experimental AIDS vaccines are tried out on monkeys. Certain experiments, however, have been less successful (at the beginning of this century a mad scientist grafted monkey sex glands into impotent patients). It is vital that the ethics of these matters be

More than a year before John Glenn became the first American to orbit the earth, on 20 February 1962, the female monkey Ham had already been put into orbit.

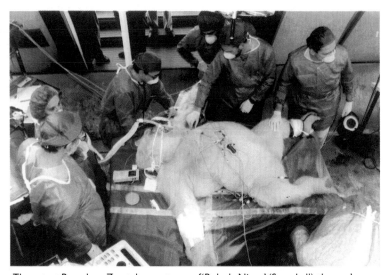

The vets at Barcelona Zoo take great care of 'Bola de Nieve' (Snowball), the zoo's mascot and the only white gorilla in the world.

The red colobus, the crested tamarin, the aye-aye... for a great many species, it's the slow road to extinction. The most threatened are undoubtedly the gorillas of Rwanda. When they are not hunted to end up as 'bush meat', their skulls get turned into lampstands and their hands are stuffed with straw to make ashtrays for tourists. Symbol of the struggle against such carnage, Dian Fossey devoted her life to their cause and was killed in 1985, probably by poachers. Her story was immortalized in the film 'Gorillas in the Mist'.

analysed, and the Dutch organization Proprimate has signed a charter aimed at giving the apes and monkeys juridical status comparable to people's rights.

Monkeys show great aptitude for 'painting'.

The monkey scholar

In contact with humans, monkeys are going through a veritable mutation. They get dressed, pampered – and their intellects are 'stimulated'. So after all the clowning and juggling, the monkey becomes a painter or a sculptor and shows a certain talent – especially since the emergence of abstract art. Scientists pore over this 'exceptionally gifted' subject and realize that it is not just capable of 'aping' humans but also knows how to solve complex problems and manipulate symbols. All it lacks is speech, and yet even here certain structures of the brain suggest a possible predisposition. Alas, the anatomy of its larynx and tongue forbid the monkey from uttering a single word. In 1966 Beatrice and Allan Gardner nevertheless established initial contact by teaching sign language to their female ape Washoe, who knew over 300 words and passed on her knowledge to her offspring without human intervention. Perhaps the dawn of a new evolution...

MONKEYS

around the world

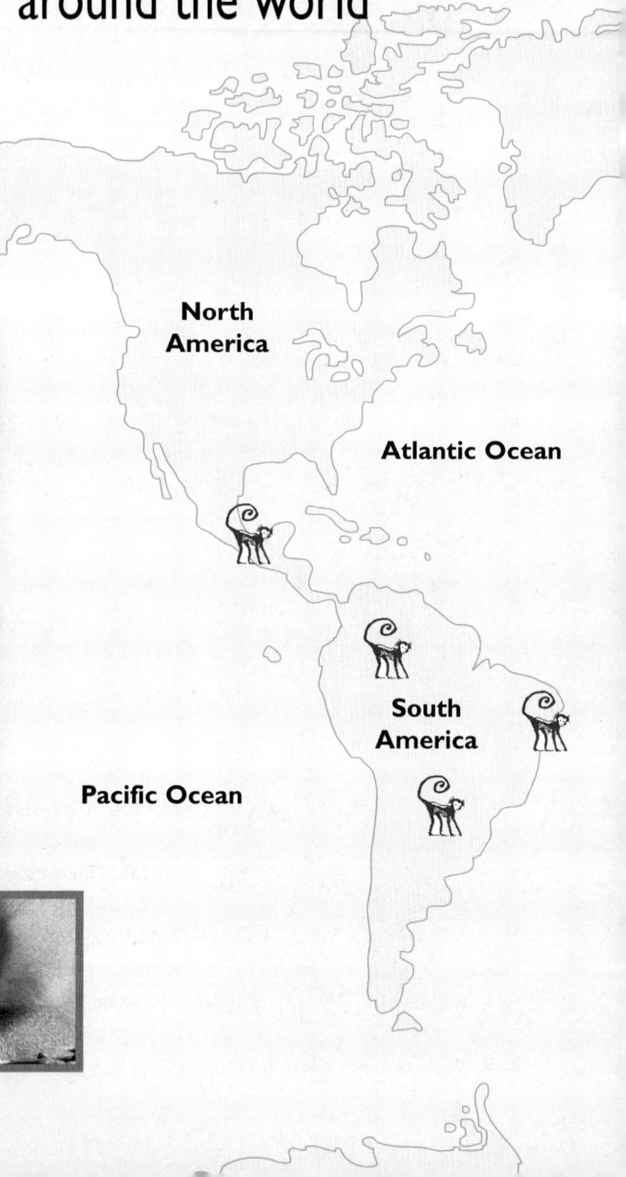

North America

Atlantic Ocean

South America

Pacific Ocean

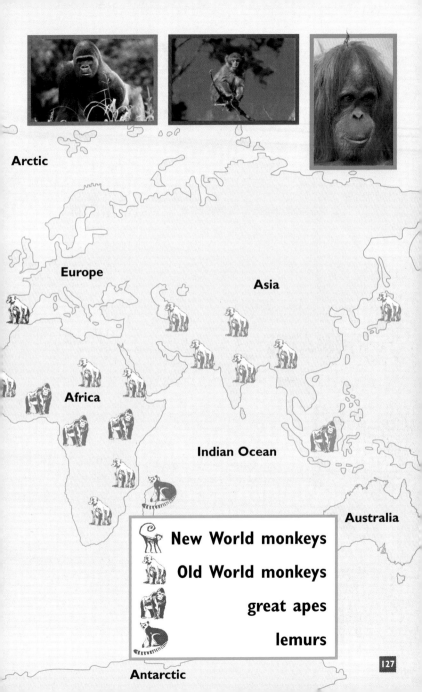

Arctic

Europe

Asia

Africa

Indian Ocean

Australia

Antarctic

New World monkeys

Old World monkeys

great apes

lemurs

127

MONKEYS

Principal Species

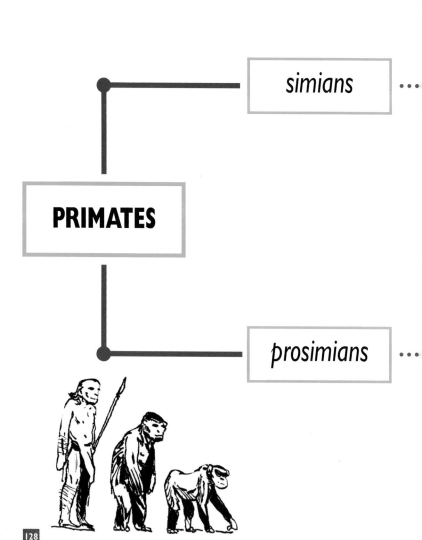

simians ...

PRIMATES

prosimians ...

Macaques, baboons and cercopithecids all have a nose with nostrils set close together.

New World monkeys have widely separated nostrils.

All anthropoid apes (chimpanzee, gorilla and orangutan) are characterised by complex behaviour.

Lemurs are the sole survivors of a formerly vast family. Today they can only be found on Madagascar.

Homo sapiens, the most bellicose and numerous among the primates, shares 90% of its genetic traits with the anthropoid apes.

Tarsiers, bushbabies and lorises have conserved amazing primitive characteristics.

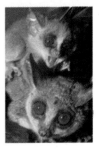

Creative workshop

*Having studied all of these creatures,
it's time to get creative.*

*All you need are a few odds and ends and a
little ingenuity, and you can incorporate
some of the animals we've seen into
beautiful craft objects.*

*These simple projects will give you further
insight into the animal kingdom presented in
the pages of this book.*

*An original and simple way to enjoy
the wonderful images of the animal kingdom.*

Lemur T-shirt

*T*he colours of this watchful lemur will stand out best on a subdued greenish-grey T-shirt.

Copying the design

• Photocopy the motif and blow it up to the desired size (1). Trace it onto the tracing paper. Turn over. Go over the reverse side with a lead pencil to

42cm

make a broad line .
• Slide the card inside the T-shirt. Fold back the excess cloth and pin it behind (2).
• Tape the tracing paper onto the T-shirt. Make a transfer of the monkey by going over the outline of the motif on the right side of the tracing.

Painting

• Next use the lead pencil to mark the divisions between the alternate white and black areas of the tail (3), and then paint the tail.
• Mix black and white to make a mid-grey. Paint the body.
• Before the grey is dry, mix the ochre-red with some grey to

132

create a gradual shading from one colour into the other and paint this over the upper part of the lemur's body.
• Paint the eyes in ochre-red.

Fixing the colours

• Let the paint dry thoroughly.
• Iron the T-shirt from the wrong side to fix the paint. Do not steam-iron.
• Do not wash the finished T-shirt at temperatures hotter than 30°C.

Materials

• A pale green cotton T-shirt • A small brush
• A small paintbrush
• Paint for painting on cloth, in black, white and ochre-red
• A sheet of A3 tracing paper • A piece of card bigger than the design
• A lead pencil
• Adhesive tape
• An iron.

Monkey Ear-rings

*T*hese two golden monkeys will dangle mischievously from your ears with as much agility as in their jungle home.

• Trace two copies of the drawing of the monkey, making one right-side and one reverse-side copy. Copy these onto the brass sheeting, pressing firmly with the lead pencil.

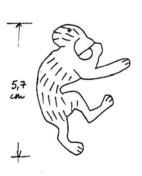

Working with the brass

• Using a pair of strong, sharp-tipped scissors, cut out each of the two monkey silhouettes. Protect the brass from scratches by placing a piece of paper over each monkey before flattening and smoothing the edges with the rounded part of the scissors.

• Mark fine lines for the fur using an awl (a knitting needle or a nail will do very well). Pierce a small hole at the top of the monkey's head by pressing harder with the awl.

Assembling the ear-rings

• Choose a few pretty coloured beads, e.g. to match the colours of your summer outfits. NB: you must be able to thread these beads

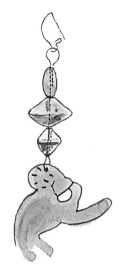

onto the brass wire when it is folded double.

• Cut a piece of brass wire, multiplying the length you want by two. Take care to leave about 8 mm extra at each end to make loops to attach it at the top and bottom.

• Thread the brass wire through the hole in the monkey's head. Fold the wire back to make a loop. Close the loop using the small pliers.

• Thread on the beads. Curve the top of the brass wire round to make a little loop and thread the ear-ring clasp through it. Close the loop with the pliers.

• Repeat for the second ear-ring, taking care to make sure the two monkeys are facing each other.

Materials

• A piece of sheet brass (available in certain arts and crafts shops) • A lead pencil • A small pair of pliers • A pair of scissors • Some glass beads (in pairs) • Brass wire • Two ear-ring clasps • A nail

Chimpanzee Jumping Jack

This jumping jack with its jointed limbs is both simple and minutely detailed.

Photocopy the patterns and blow them up: the monkey's head should measure six centimetres in length.

Preparing the patterns

• Hold the photocopy inside the cardboard box with your finger-tips, spray the reverse side of the sheet lightly with glue and place it on the plywood.

Preparing the pieces

Clamp the sheet of wood firmly to a workbench or to a corner of the kitchen table, taking care to protect it from marking. Saw round the black outline (1), turning the wood as you go. Repeat for all the limbs. When you cut out the front and back of the body, put two pieces of wood one on top of the other and cut them together to that the two pieces are identical. • Cut three little chocks 1.2 cm on a side out of the thicker piece of plywood. • Drill holes through the tops of the thighs and through the shoulders as shown on the pattern, using the 2 mm bit. • Sand down the surfaces and the edges of all the pieces with sandpaper. • Dye them on one side and on the edge,

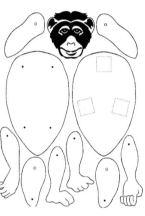

applying the dye in a single even coat (2). Place them on three or four upturned drawing-pins to dry.

The arms and legs

• Place the left upper arm and left lower arm so that the elbow ends of both are together. Place a small board under-neath, then drive a tack through both parts at the black dot so that they are nailed together. Use the pliers to bend the end of the tack over where it sticks out and finally flatten it at right-angles against the wood with the hammer (4), then open out the assembled limb. Repeat for the other arm, then for the legs.

The front and back of the body

• Following the pattern, glue the three chocks onto the 'underside' of the body. Weight them down with a thick, heavy book and wait for them to dry. Place a drop of glue on each before proceeding to the next step. • To protect the table, before nailing the front and back of the body together place the

'underside' of the body on a sheet of thick cardboard or on a piece of scrap wood so that the holes do not go all the way through to the table.

• Drive tacks though the black dots on the 'upper side' of the body so that they stick out a little. Assemble by positioning the 'upper side' on the 'underside' of the body. There will still be a 1 mm gap left when you slide in the four limbs and fasten them with the tacks which you have driven lightly into place (5). • Make sure that the limbs can move freely, and finish driving the tacks right in. Use the cutting edge of the pliers or a hacksaw to cut off the tips where they stick out, and sand down. Touch up with dye if the colouring has been damaged.

The head

• Spread glue on the lower two thirds of one side of the head. Assemble by placing on the front side of the body so that it sticks out some way above the shoulders. Wipe off any excess glue with a cloth. Place on a flat surface protected with a sheet of paper, weight down with a heavy book and wait for it to dry.

Finish

• Glue a picture hook to the back. Hang up.

Materials

• Two plywood off-cuts, one 3 mm thick measuring 20 x 25 cm and the other 3.5 or 4 mm thick and measuring 1.2 x 3.6 cm • A glue spray with directional nozzle • A cardboard box • A hand fret-saw or an electric jigsaw: in either case, use a fine blade • A clamp • Sandpaper • Brown wood-dye or ink • A medium-sized paintbrush • Some drawing-pins • A gimlet with a 2 mm diameter bit • Another, finer gimlet. • White wood glue • Round-headed brass tacks 12 mm long, with heads 1.3 mm in diameter • A hammer • A pair of fine-nosed universal pliers

Monkey Magnets

*W*ith these easy-to-make rubber magnets, anyone can create these stylised monkeys for sticking don't-forget notes to the fridge door or for decoration.

For the patterns

• Of course you may prefer to create your own figures.
• To copy these figures, place a sheet of tracing paper on the pieces for the designs you have chosen and use the lead pencil to trace each shape onto the paper. Turn the paper over and go over

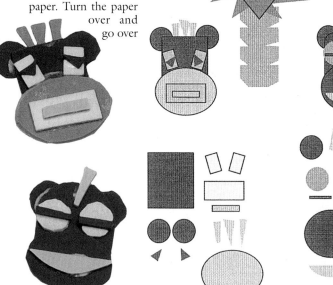

• Cut out the various shapes with the scissors.

• Glue them together, one on top of another as shown: the background must contrast with the details. Use a solvent-free glue which will not dissolve the rubber and is safe for children to handle.

• Wait patiently for the figures to dry before handling them.

• Stick a small magnet onto the back of each figure to create a decorative fridge magnet.

the outlines to leave a broad line. Turn the paper right side up again and place it on the different coloured sheets of rubber, then go over the shapes again in pencil. Take care to copy only the pieces of the appropriate colour onto each sheet.

Materials

• A sheet of tracing paper • A fairly soft lead pencil (B) • Five sheets of rubber for cutting out (available from certain arts and crafts shops), in brown, beige, green, yellow and pink • A pair of scissors • Solvent-free glue • Small magnets (available from certain arts and crafts shops)

Acknowledgements:

The publishers would like to thank all those who have contributed to this book,
in particular:
Guy-Claude Agboton, Evelyne-Alice Bridier, Antoine Caron, Jean-Jacques Carreras,
Michèle Forest, Nicolas Lemaire, Hervé Levano, Marie-Bénédicte Majoral,
Kha Luan Pham, Vincent Pompougnac, Marie-Laure Sers-Besson,
Valérie Zuber, Emmanuèle Zumstein

Illustration: Frantz Rey

Translation: Kate Clayton, Ros Schwartz Translations

Impression: Eurolitho - Milan
Dépôt légal: September 1998
Printed in Italy